Field Journal Snqeymintn

Name

Date

Field Journal ✦ Snqeymintn

A Component of the Explore the River Educational Project

Confederated Salish and Kootenai Tribes

University of Nebraska Press | Lincoln and London

The title of this field journal, *Snqeymintn*, is a Salish Indian word that translates as "a place where you write something".

The Explore the River Project

This field journal is one part of a larger bull trout restoration and protection project. The project includes an integrated set of educational materials that focus not only on the Confederated Salish and Kootenai Tribes' restoration and management efforts, but also on bull trout, their habitat needs, and their historic relationship to the Salish, Kootenai, and Pend d'Oreille people. The materials also discuss key hydrological and ecological concepts fundamental to restoration; the changes that have occurred in aquatic and riparian habitats as a result of one hundred years of agriculture, irrigation, and grazing practices; and how and why restoration is occurring in the Jocko watershed. In addition to this field journal, it includes a storybook for students entitled *Bull Trout's Gift*, an interactive DVD designed primarily for middle and high school students entitled *Explore the River*, a website targeting the general public, and a curriculum guide for educators.

Credits

Elder quotations provided by the Salish-Pend d'Oreille Culture Committee (SPCC). The Louise McDonald quotation is from an interview recorded in 1988 for The Place of Falling Water film project. Other Salish-Pend d'Oreille elder quotations are from interviews recorded in 2006 for the Explore the River Project. Salish plant, fish, and wildlife names provided by the SPCC, with special thanks to Thompson Smith. Salish names for fishing implements provided by Steven M. Egesdal. Front and back cover and title page watercolors by Sashay Carnel. Fish illustrations by Joseph Tomelleri. Other illustration and photo credits as follows: David Rockwell - pgs 4, 38, 50, 62, 70 (trap constructed by Tim Ryan), 82; Mary Vaux Walcott - pgs 5, 7, 14, 30, 58, 66, 86; American Museum of Natural History - pgs 22, 94, 98; SPCC: pg 46; National Geographic Society - pg 78; G.D. Ehret - pg 6; Adeleene Rockwell - pg 42.

This project is made possible through the generous support of the Confederated Salish and Kootenai Tribes' Jocko River Restoration Fund.

♾

Library of Congress Cataloging-in-Publication Data

Field journal Snqeymintn : a component of the Explore the River Educational Project / Confederated Salish and Kootenai Tribes.
        p. cm.
ISBN 978-0-8032-3528-1 (paper : alk. paper)
1. Natural history—Fieldwork—Montana—Jocko River Region. 2. Animals—Montana—Jocko River Region. 3. Plants—Montana—Jocko River Region.
4. Fishes—Montana—Jocko River. 5. Jocko River Region (Mont.)—Environmental conditions. 6. Confederated Salish & Kootenai Tribes of the Flathead Reservation, Montana—Environmental conditions. 7. Stream conservation—Montana—Jocko River. 8. Bull trout—Conservation—Montana—Jocko River.
9. Salish language—Pronunciation. 10. Kalispel language—Pronunciation. I. Explore the River Educational Project. II. Confederated Salish & Kootenai Tribes of the Flathead Reservation, Montana. III. Title: Snqeymintn.
QH105.M9F54 2011   508.786'83—dc22   2010046305

Contents

ƚʔay
(small bull trout)

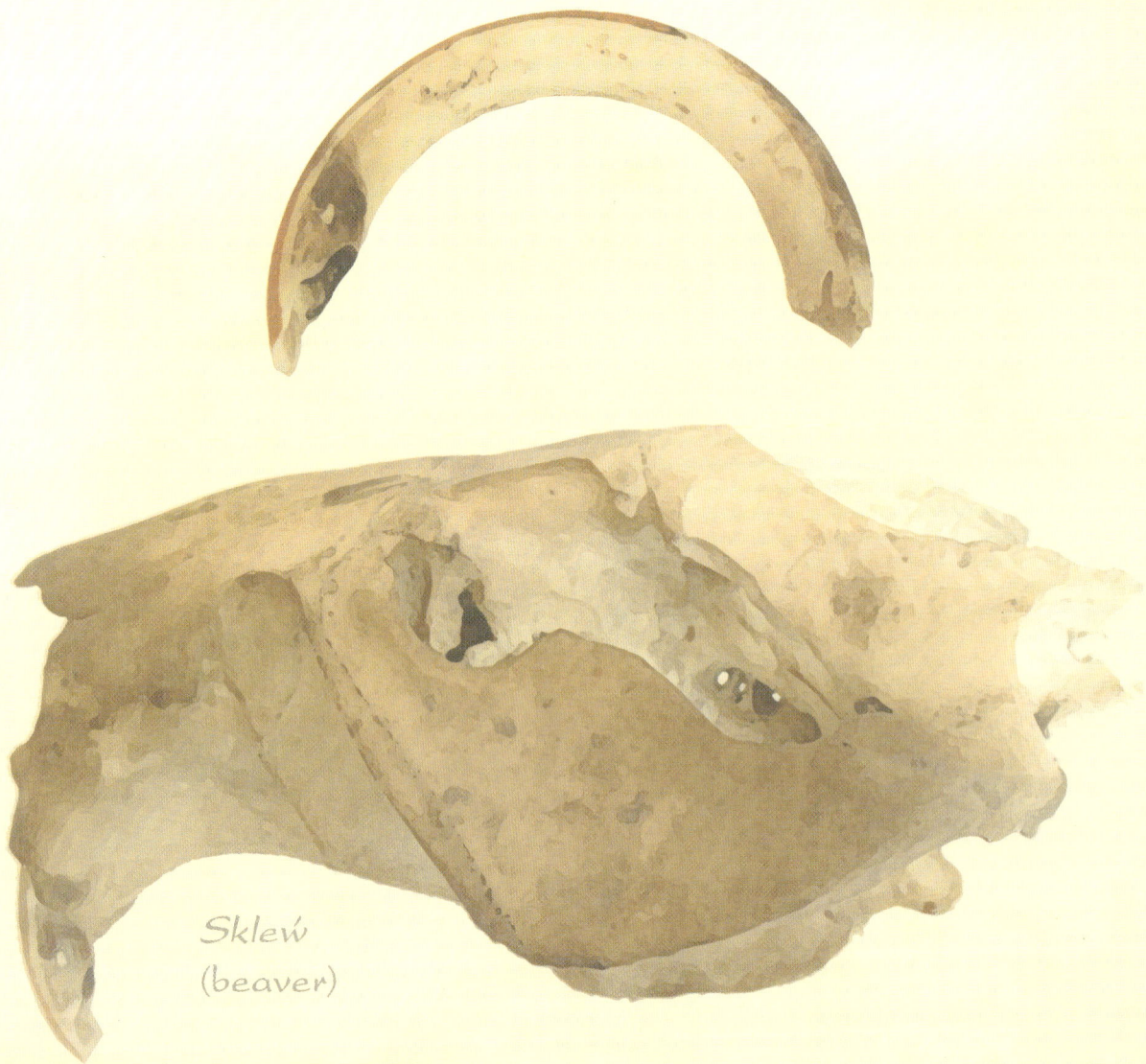

Skleẃ
(beaver)

Riparian Animals of the Jocko River

Reptiles and Amphibians

Long-toed salamander
Rocky Mountain tailed frog
Western toad
Pacific chorus frog
Northern leopard frog

Columbia spotted frog
Painted turtle
Western skink
Northern alligator lizard
Rubber boa

Gopher snake
Terrestrial garter snake
Common garter snake
Eastern racer
Prairie rattlesnake

Birds

Great blue heron
Tundra swan
Trumpeter swan
Canada goose
Wood duck
Green-winged teal
Mallard
Northern pintail
Blue-winged teal
Cinnamon teal
Northern shoveler
American wigeon
Canvasback
Redhead
Lesser scaup

Common goldeneye
Gadwall
American white pelican
Ring-necked duck
Barrow's goldeneye
Bufflehead
Hooded merganser
Common merganser
Osprey
Bald eagle
Cooper's hawk
Red-tailed hawk
Peregrine falcon
Ruffed grouse
Wild turkey

Double-crested cormorant
Merlin
American kestrel
Killdeer
Ring-billed gull
American coot
Spotted sandpiper
Rock pigeon
Mourning dove
W. Screech owl
Great horned owl
Long eared owl
Northern saw-whet owl
Black-chinned hummingbird

Qʷq̓ʷtqnetp
(fireweed)

Rufous hummingbird
Northern pygmy-owl
Common nighthawk
Calliope hummingbird
Belted kingfisher
Downy woodpecker
Hairy woodpecker
Northern flicker
Pileated woodpecker
Willow flycatcher
Eastern kingbird
Cliff swallow
Barn swallow
Steller's jay
Black-billed magpie
American crow
Common raven
Clark's nutcracker
Western peewee
Tree swallow

N. rough-winged swallow
Bank swallow
Warbling vireo
Pygmy nuthatch
Ruby-crowned kinglet
Golden-crowned kinglet
Black-capped chickadee
Mountain chickadee
Chestnut-backed chickadee
White-breasted nuthatch
Brown creeper
House wren
Winter wren
Dipper
Townsend's solitaire
Swainson's thrush
Hermit thrush
American robin
Varied thrush
Gray catbird

Mountain bluebird
Western bluebird
Bohemian waxwing
Cedar waxwing
Cassin's vireo
Red-eyed vireo
Red-breasted nuthatch
Orange-crowned warbler
Nashville warbler
Yellow warbler
Yellow-rumped warbler
Townsend's warbler
American redstart
Northern waterthrush
Macgillivray's warbler
Common yellowthroat
Wilson's warbler
Yellow-breasted chat
Black-headed grosbeak

American tree sparrow
Chipping sparrow
Western tanager
Yellow headed blackbird
Lazuli bunting
Spotted towhee
Fox sparrow
Song sparrow
Lincoln's sparrow
White-throated sparrow
White-crowned sparrow
Dark eyed junco
Red-winged blackbird
Bullock's oriole
Cassin's finch
House finch
American goldfinch
Pine siskin
Evening grosbeak
Pine grosbeak

Mammals

Dusky shrew
Vagrant shrew
Water shrew
Mountain cottontail

Northern flying squirrel
Red squirrel
Yellow-pine chipmunk
Beaver

Deer mouse
Bushy-tailed woodrat
Meadow vole
Long-tailed vole

Muskrat
Porcupine
Coyote
Gray wolf

Neelo
(shootingstar)

Red fox
Black bear
Grizzly bear
Short-tailed weasel
Long-tailed weasel
Mink

Pine Marten
Striped skunk
River otter
Bobcat
Mountain lion
Elk

White-tailed deer
Moose
Silver-haired bat
Fringed myotis
Long-eared myotis
Long-legged myotis

California myotis
Little brown myotis

Selected Common Riparian Plants of the Jocko River

Trees

Black cottonwood
Quaking aspen
Ponderosa pine
Rocky Mountain juniper

Shrubs

Alder
Serviceberry
Oregon-grape
Water birch
Red-osier dogwood
Black hawthorn
Mock orange
American plum

Chokecherry
Prickly current
Wood's rose
Red raspberry
Bebb willow
Drummond willow
Sandbar willow
Blue elderberry
Snowberry

Forbs

Common yarrow
Dogbane
Fireweed
Large-leaved avens
American licorice

Cow parsnip
Lupine
Indian paintbrush
Field mint
Goldenrod

Graminoids (grasses and grasslike plants)

Bluebunch wheatgrass
Nebraska sedge
Beaked sedge
Mannagrass
Baltic rush
Bulrush

Selected Native Fish of the Jocko River

Aay
Large Bull Trout

Pist
Westslope Cutthroat Trout

Łʔay
Small Bull Trout

X̣ʷy̓ú
Mountain Whitefish

Q̓ʷq̓ʷé
Northern Pikeminnow

Slaẃs
Largescale Sucker

P̓ič̓l
Redside Shiner

Čléneʔ
Longnose Sucker

Sttm̓a
Slimy Sculpin

Field Observations

Date/Time of Day: _____

Accompanied by: _____

Location: _____

Weather: _____

Type of Habitat: _____

_____

Condition of Habitat: _____

_____

Fun or Interesting Observations: _____

_____

_____

_____

_____

_____

_____

Species Seen: _____

_____

Sttma
(slimy sculpin)

Sketches, Poems, Songs, or Thoughts

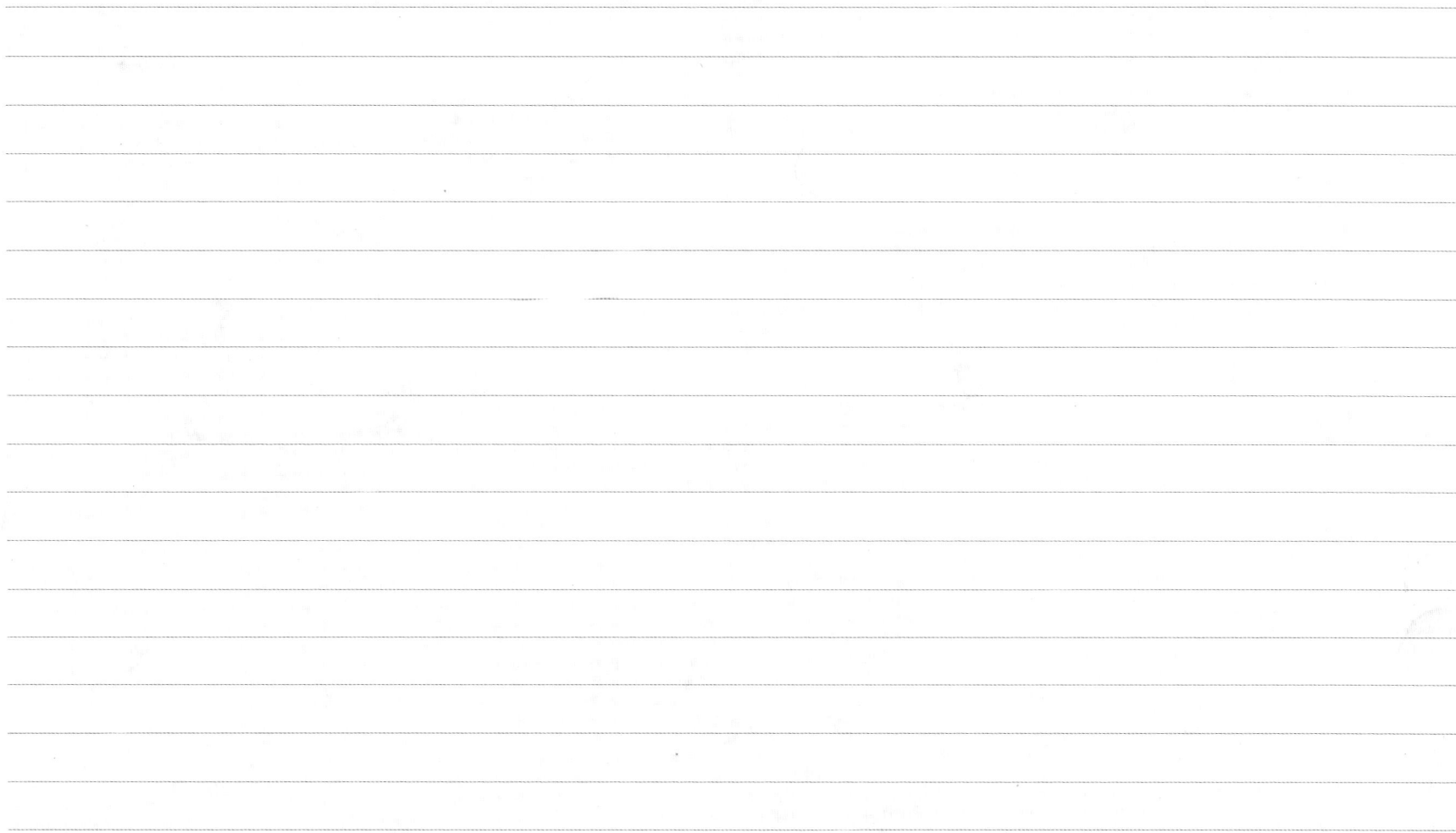

In the beginning, when I saw this land, it was beautiful.

This land was good...All our waters, our creeks were flowing along

good...It is there in the water — that is where there were many animals

— fish and other things. And by that, we were wealthy from the water...

— Mitch Smallsalmon, 1977

(Salish-Pend d'Oreille Culture Committee)

Stmtu
(prickly currant)

In the springtime, when the snow melts, they would select the ones who will pray, the ones who are strong...They said, "All of you go, you're going to bless the streams, the spring waters from these mountains. Go to a stream, to where it begins. You will pray, pray for that stream, that it never dries up, that it won't get dirty, that the water will always be good."

— Pat Pierre, 2006

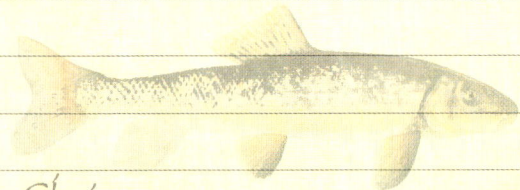

Slaws
(largescale sucker)

There used to be a lot of fish. There was big

whitefish and trout.

— Pete Beaverhead, 1975

(Salish-Pend d'Oreille Culture Committee)

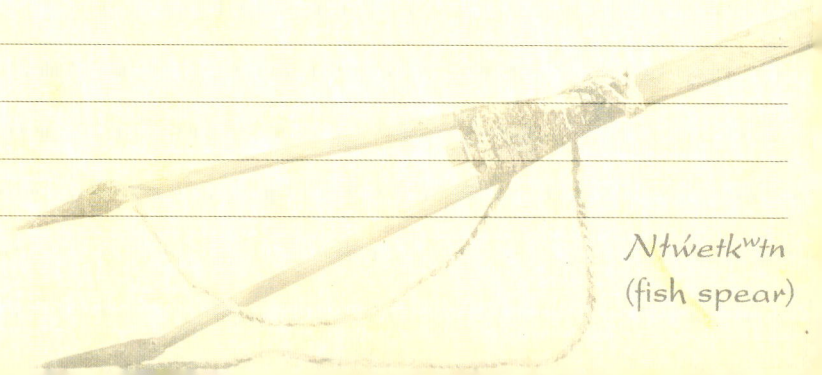

Ntwetkʷtn
(fish spear)

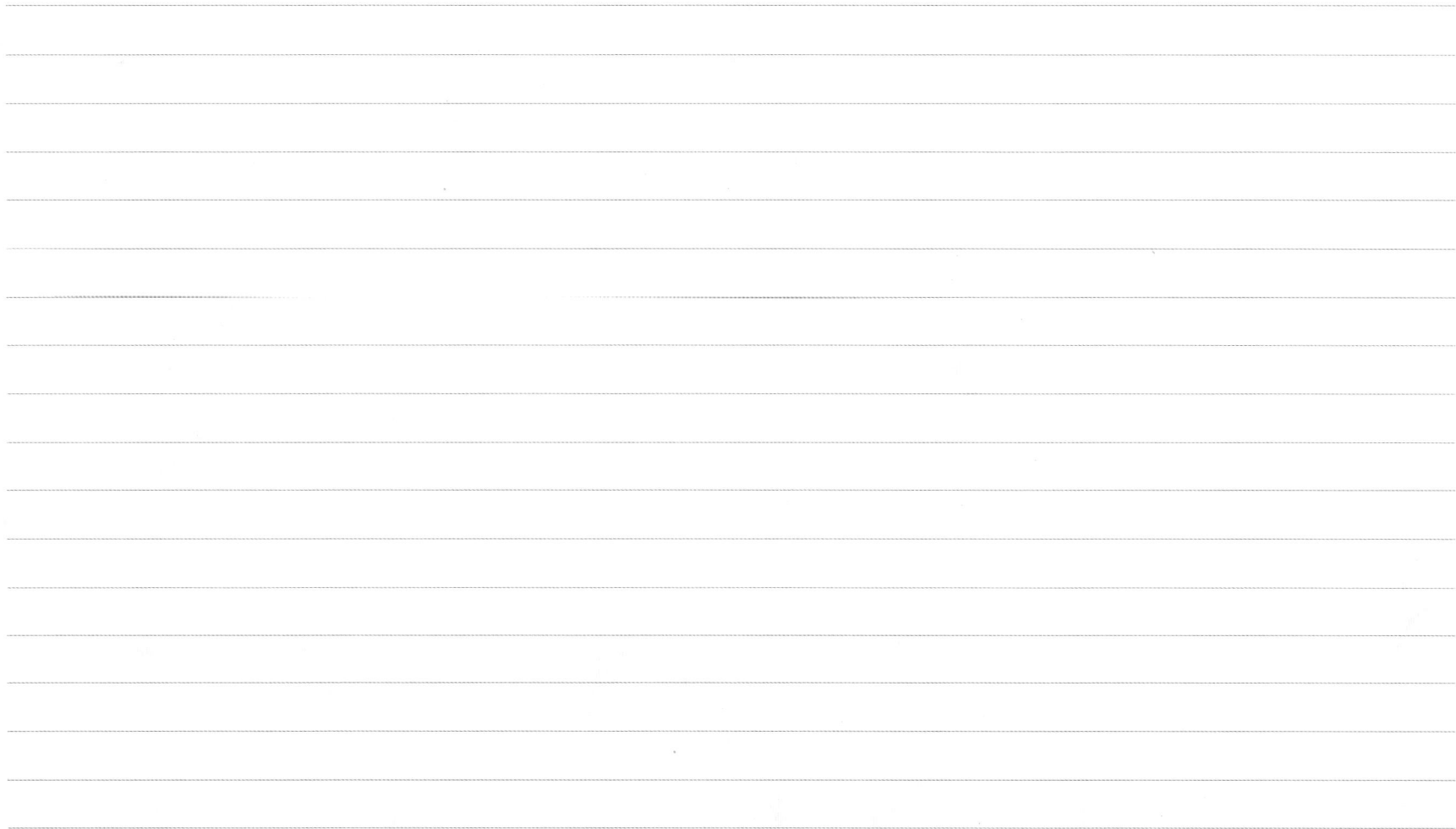

They made use of everything.

They never threw anything away....

— Louise Vanderburg 1975

(Salish-Pend d'Oreille Culture Committee)

x̣ʷýú
(mountain whitefish)

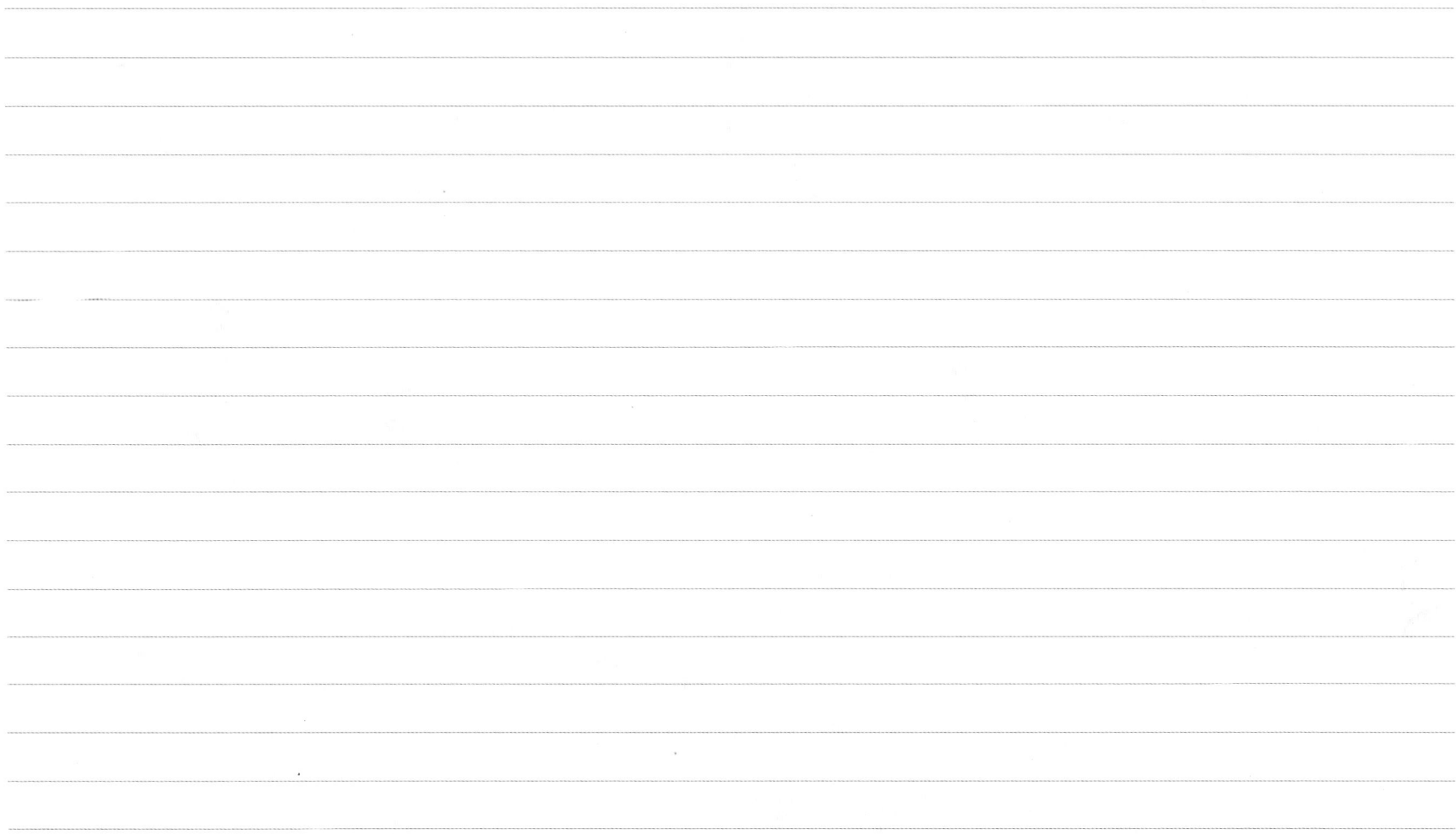

When we gather anything from the land, we give something

back. It's like we trade for something. We thank our Mother

Earth. Give something back...that's your thanks.

— Pat Pierre, 2006

Słaq
(serviceberry)

We'd go to the river to fish. If not there, then at Jocko Lake,

St. Mary's Lake...there were a lot of fish...whenever you had

enough, then that would be it. We didn't waste.

— Mary "Dolly" Linsebigler, 2006

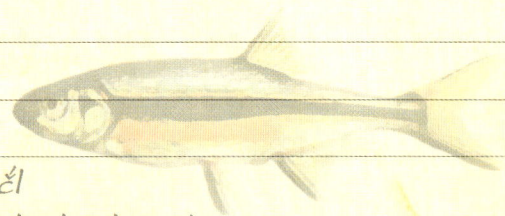

Píčl
(redside shiner)

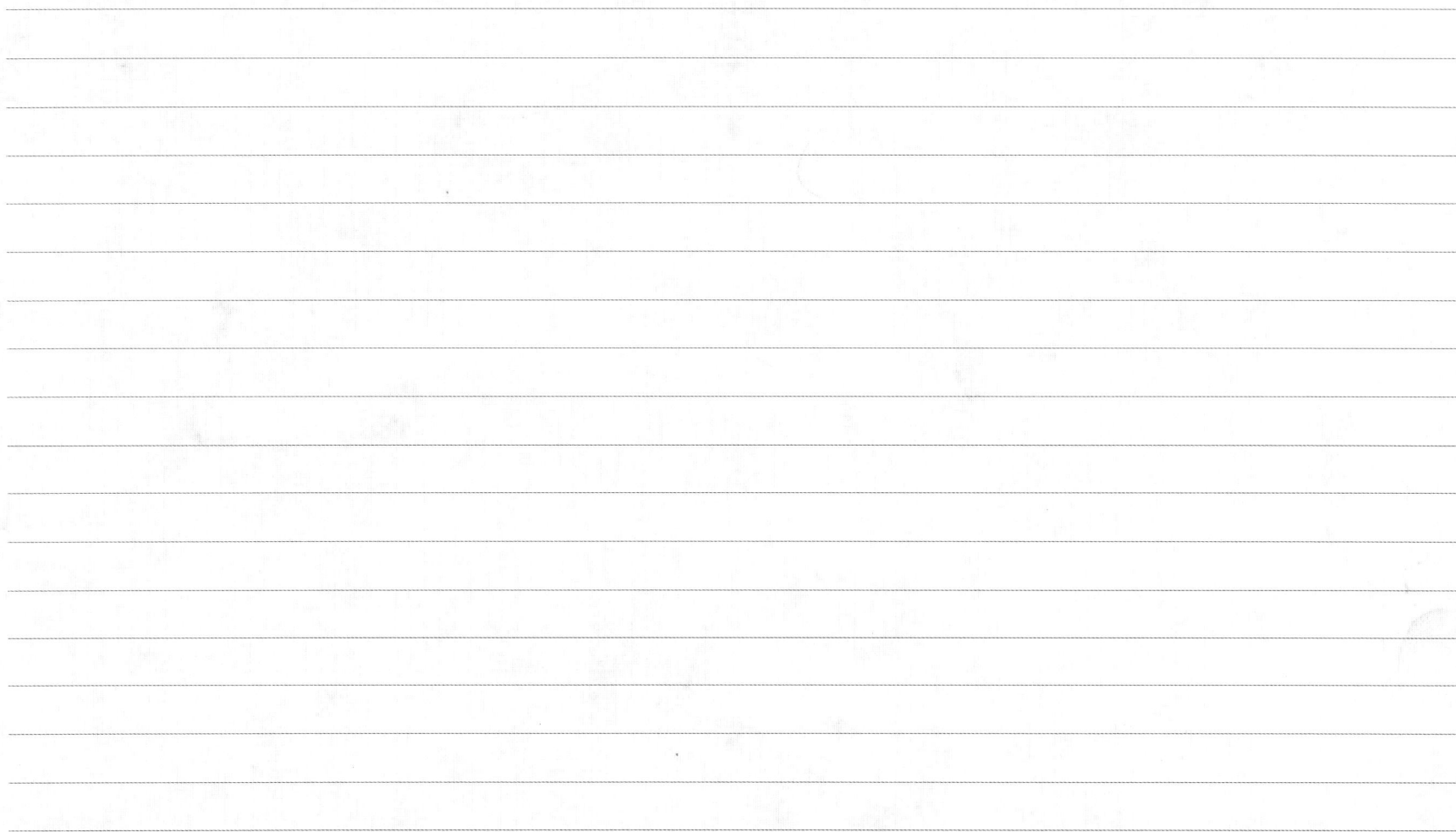

You need bull trout not only for food, but for our culture, for our

stories, for our spirituality.

— Antoine "Tony" Incashola, 2006

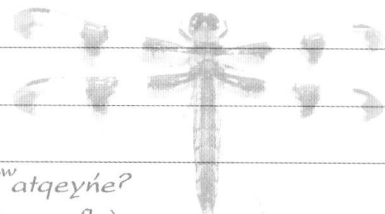

X̣ʷatqeyńeʔ
(dragonfly)

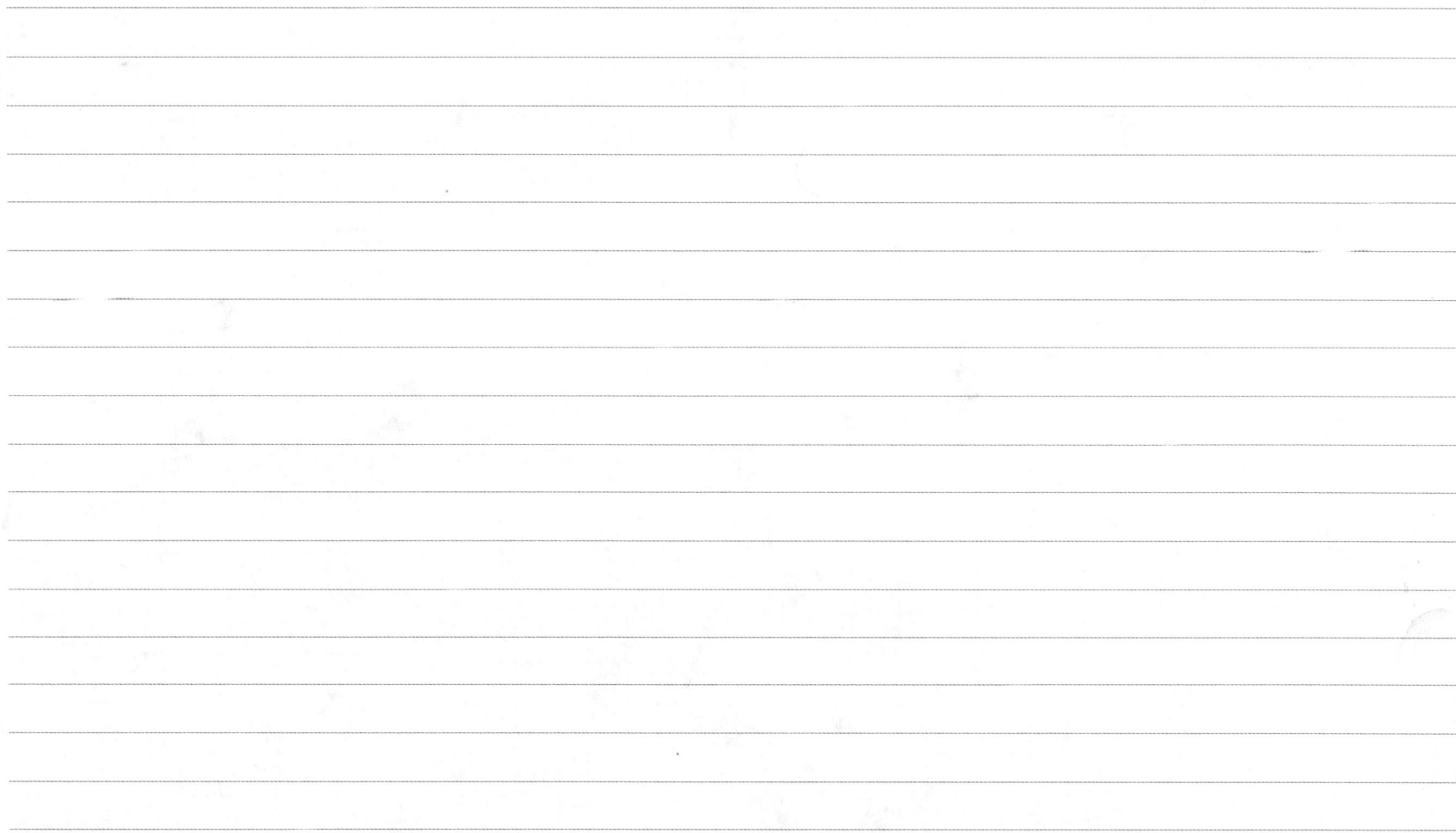

Take special care of our water. A long time ago, wherever there

was a stream flowing, you could drink the water.

Today, it seems, we're fearful of...the water.

— Mary "Dolly" Linsebigler, 2006

Ƙʷelu
(butterfly)

I think it was in the late 1940s that I realized the water was

changing. At first when we'd swim, there used to be a lot of

freshwater mussels...It was then that we noticed the mussel

shells were opened. From that time on, the mussels began

dying out. I didn't know why because I was a child.

— Michael Durglo Sr., 2006

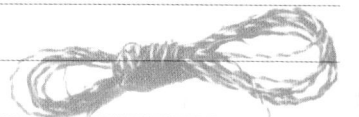

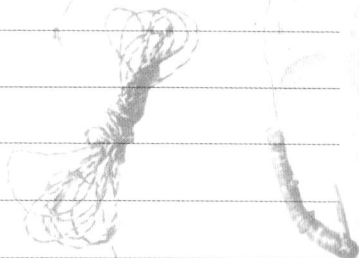

Čálxʷé
(fish hooks)

That was our road, the river, used by our elders, our ancestors.

A long time ago, they always traveled by the water.

— Pat Pierre, 2006

Čťáqnšn
(stonefly nymph)

In all that we did water was included. My elders — my maternal

grandfathers, my paternal grandfathers, my maternal

grandmothers — and so to us children, to all of us,

our relatives, water was priceless.

— Mary "Dolly" Linsebigler, 2006

Pist
(westslope cutthroat)

That's what you should do, my children, that's what you should
remember. Our ancestors' way of life...I don't want it to quit, to
be no more, our customs here on earth.

—Mitch Smallsalmon

(Salish-Pend d'Oreille Culture Committee)

Ṃtčẃe
(arrowleaf balsamroot)

There used to be plenty of bull trout. They were all big.

For us it was just a common fish. We never thought

bull trout might disappear.

— Pat Pierre, 2006

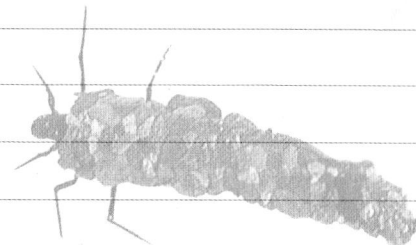

Ččnčpi
(caddisfly larvae)

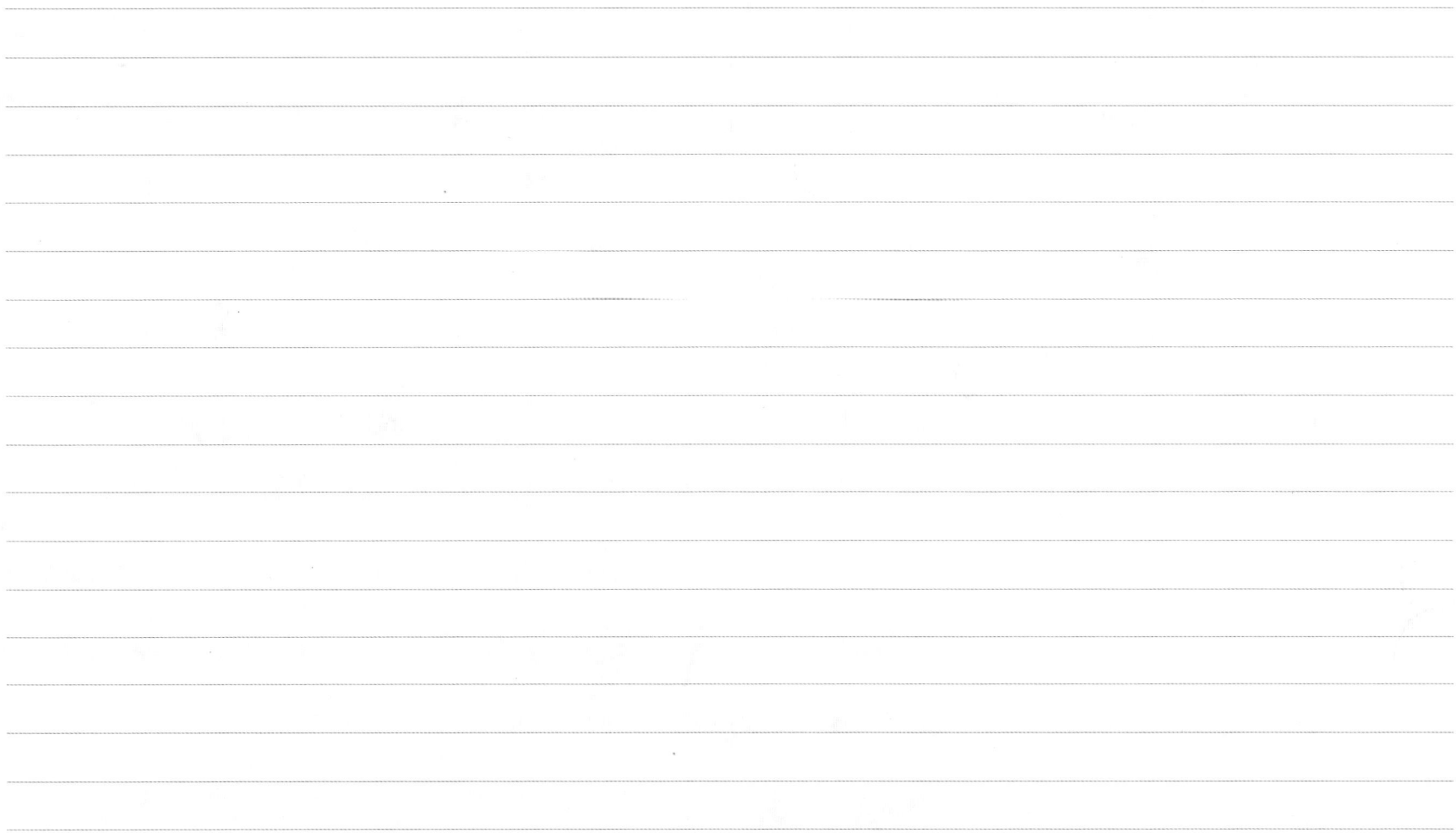

We didn't only use fishing poles. We speared fish. We snagged

fish. We trapped fish. We had many ways to catch fish for our

fellow tribal people. It's not only our food.

It's like our medicine also.

— Michael Durglo Sr., 2006

Seč
(nodding onion)

Fishing, to me at least, is not a sport. It is still an art of survival,

of something that our culture as Indian people depend on.

— Antoine "Tony" Incashola, 2006

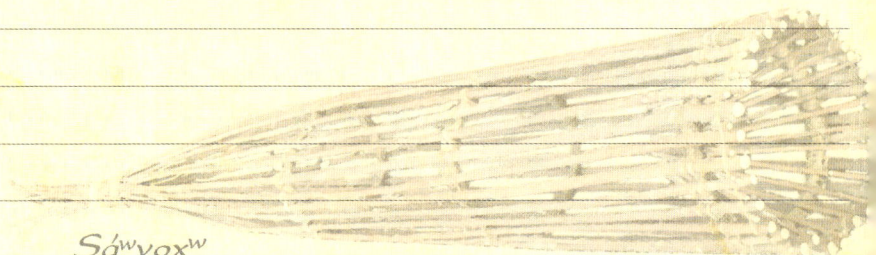

Sq̓ʷyoẋʷ
Fish trap

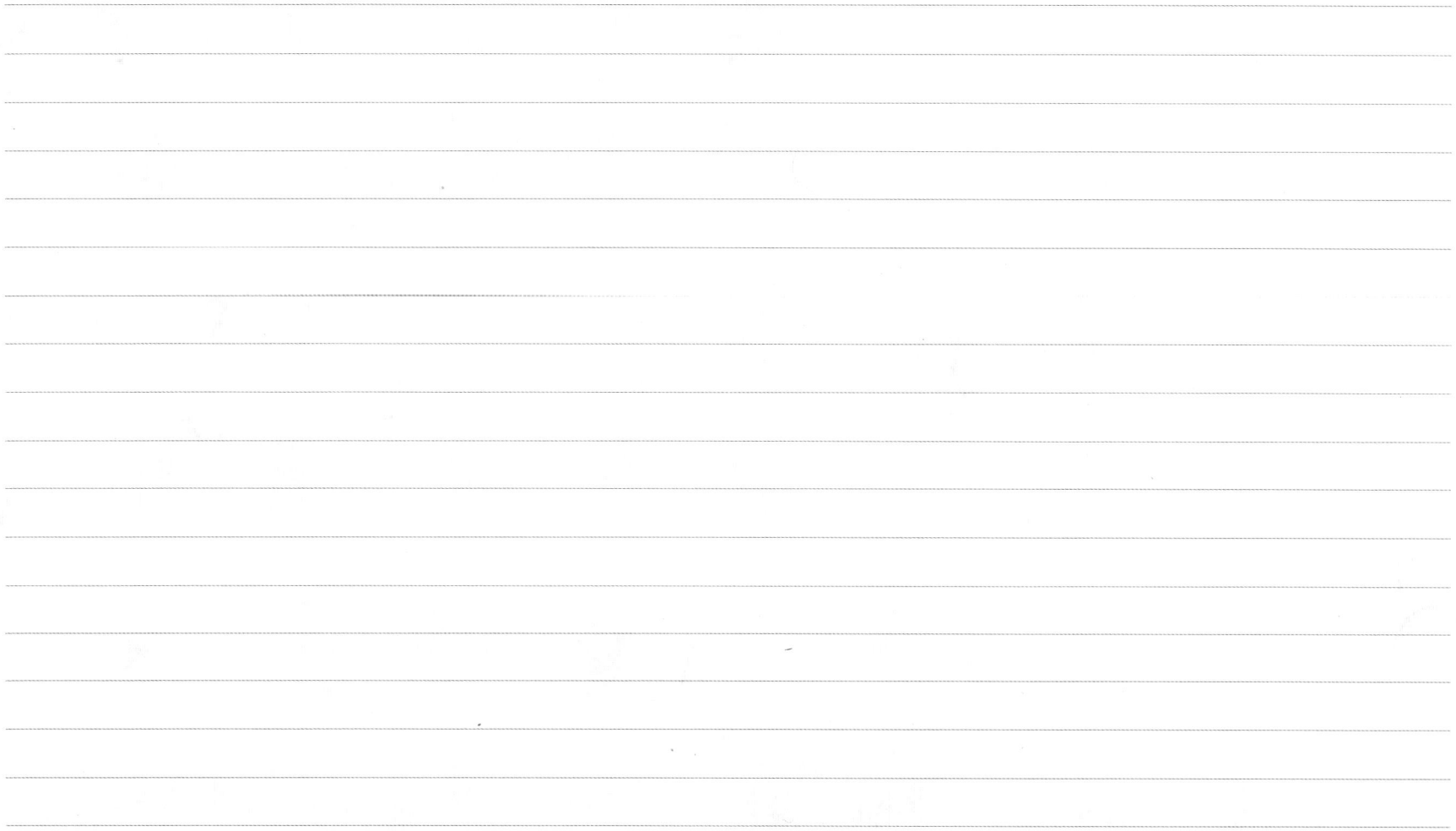

Once in a while I go to the river. I sit on the shore; I listen to the

water. Later I hear a song, once in a while a beautiful song. It

passes by. I think I want to remember that song [but] I forget it;

it passes by. That is the water. It passes by.

It never stops.

— Pat Pierre, 2006

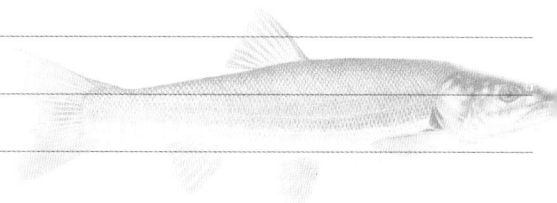

$Q^w \acute{q}^w \acute{e}$
(northern pikeminnow)

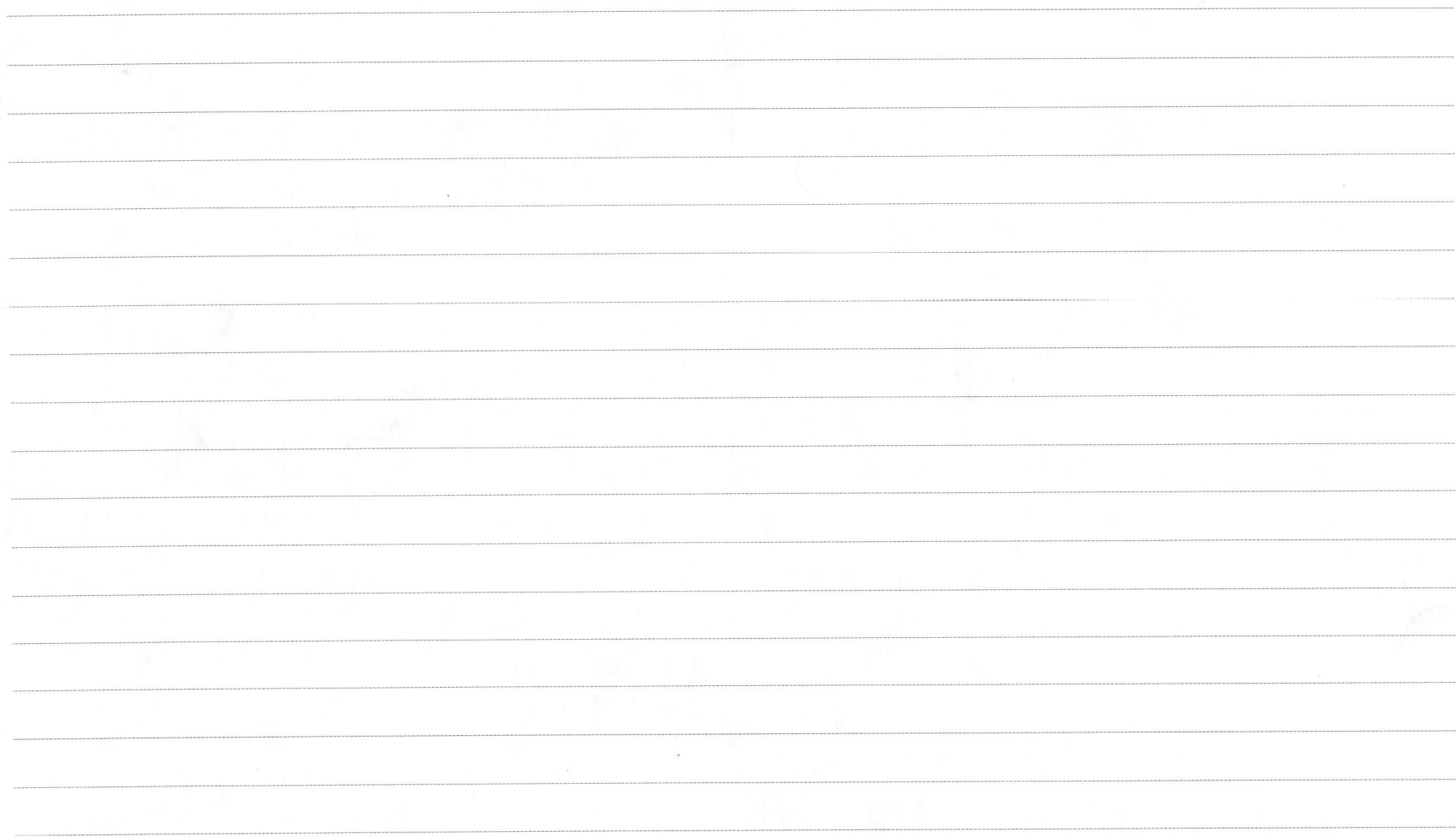

A long time ago we were told by the elders,

"If you misuse anything it will be gone.

You'll be in need of it, you'll be in need for water or whatever,

if you don't take care of it."

— Mary "Dolly" Linsebigler, 2006

Sćals
(oregon-grape)

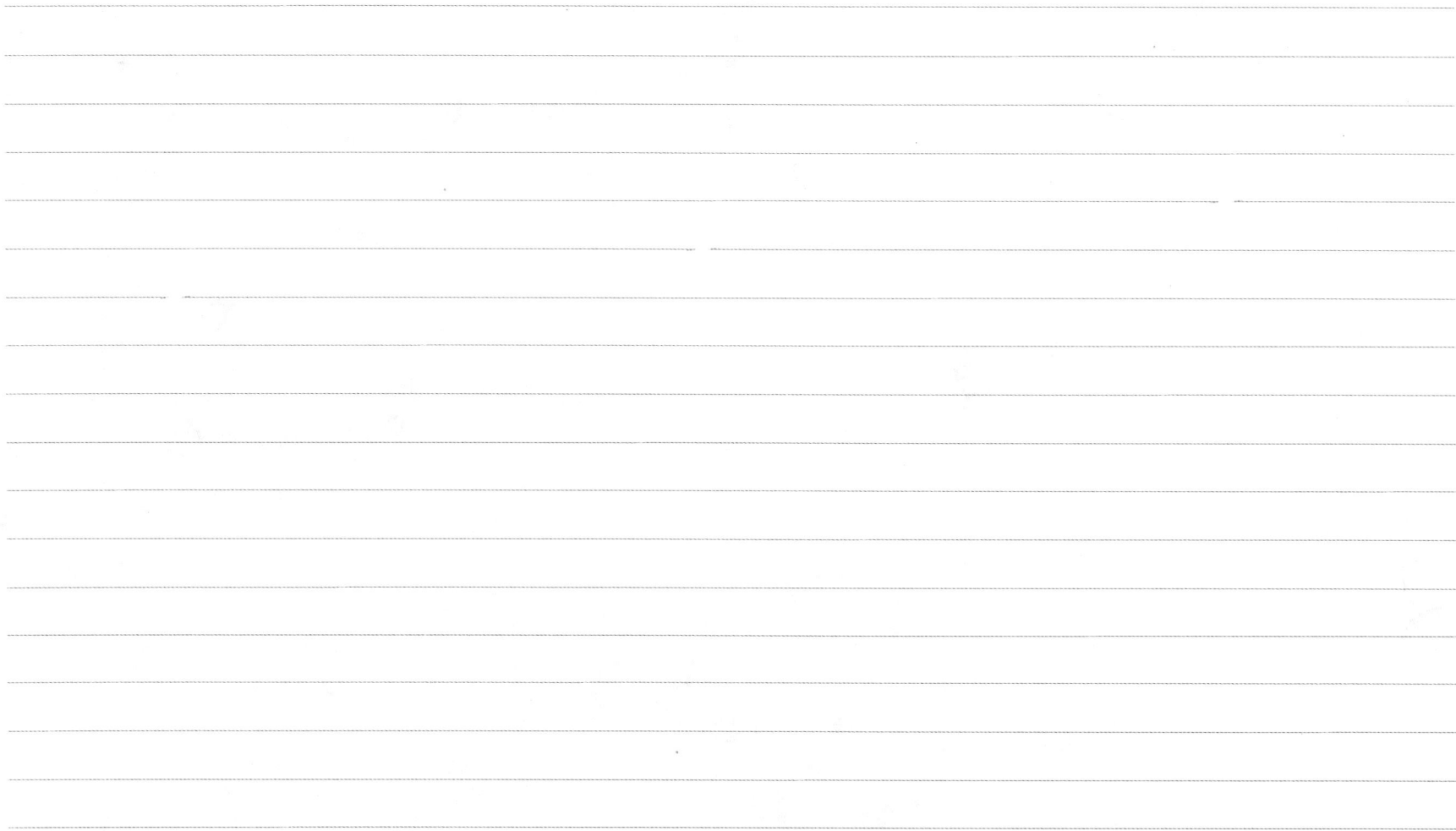

They put too many different kinds of fish in the creeks and rivers.

I think that's how it goes nowadays. They put fish here and there.

Now our old fish are gone.

— Louise McDonald, 1988

Skʷk̓ʷlaɬeʔ
(western pearlshell mussel)

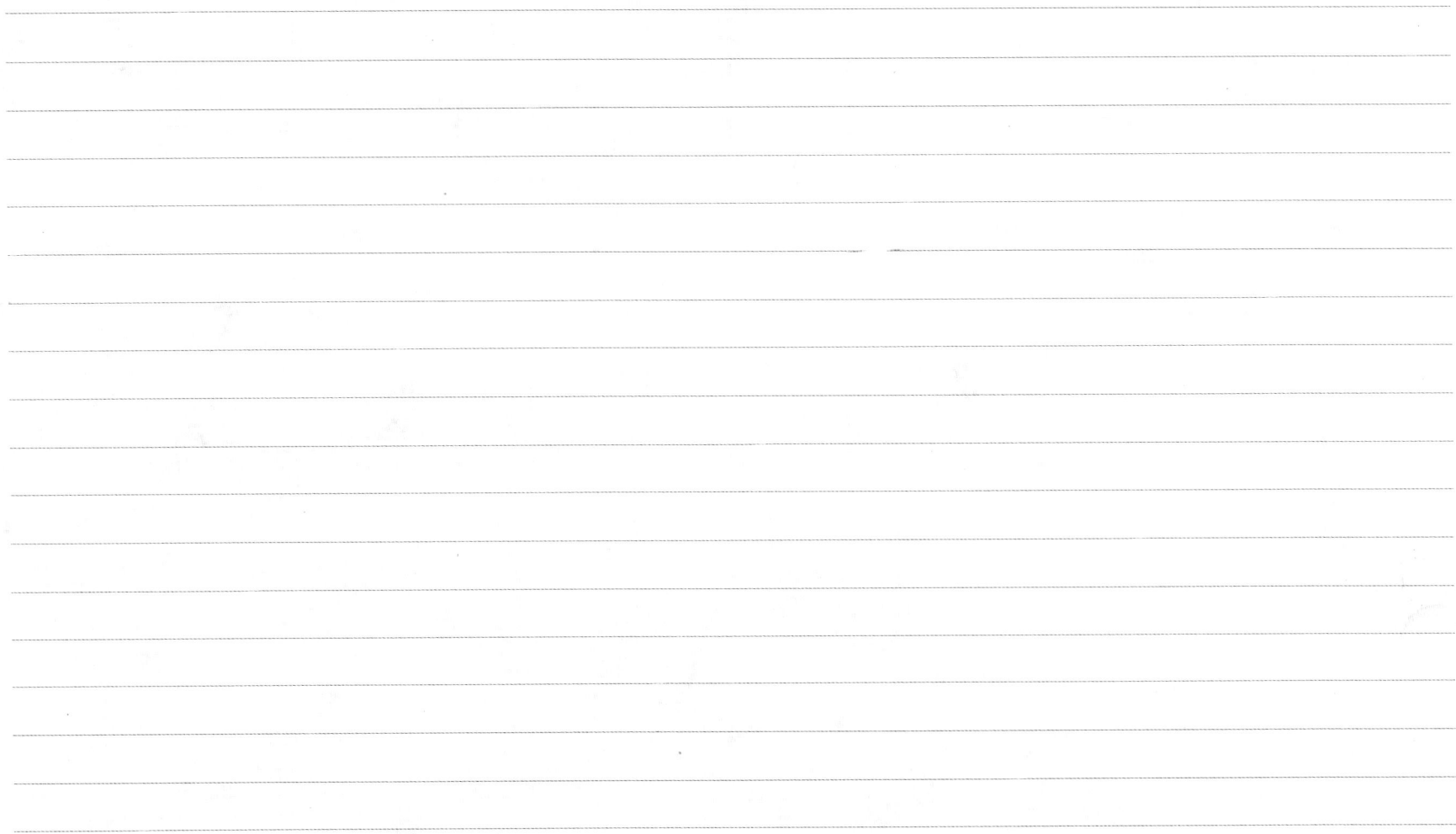

When I was still small...it was our job to do the fishing. We would [catch] a lot of fish and these would be dried. Gutted and dried. When we'd get a lot, then my paternal grandmother would fix it, dry them and put them away, like deer meat, saved until winter. It's food. The fish was important.

— Pat Pierre, 2006

Pólplqn
(thimbleberry)

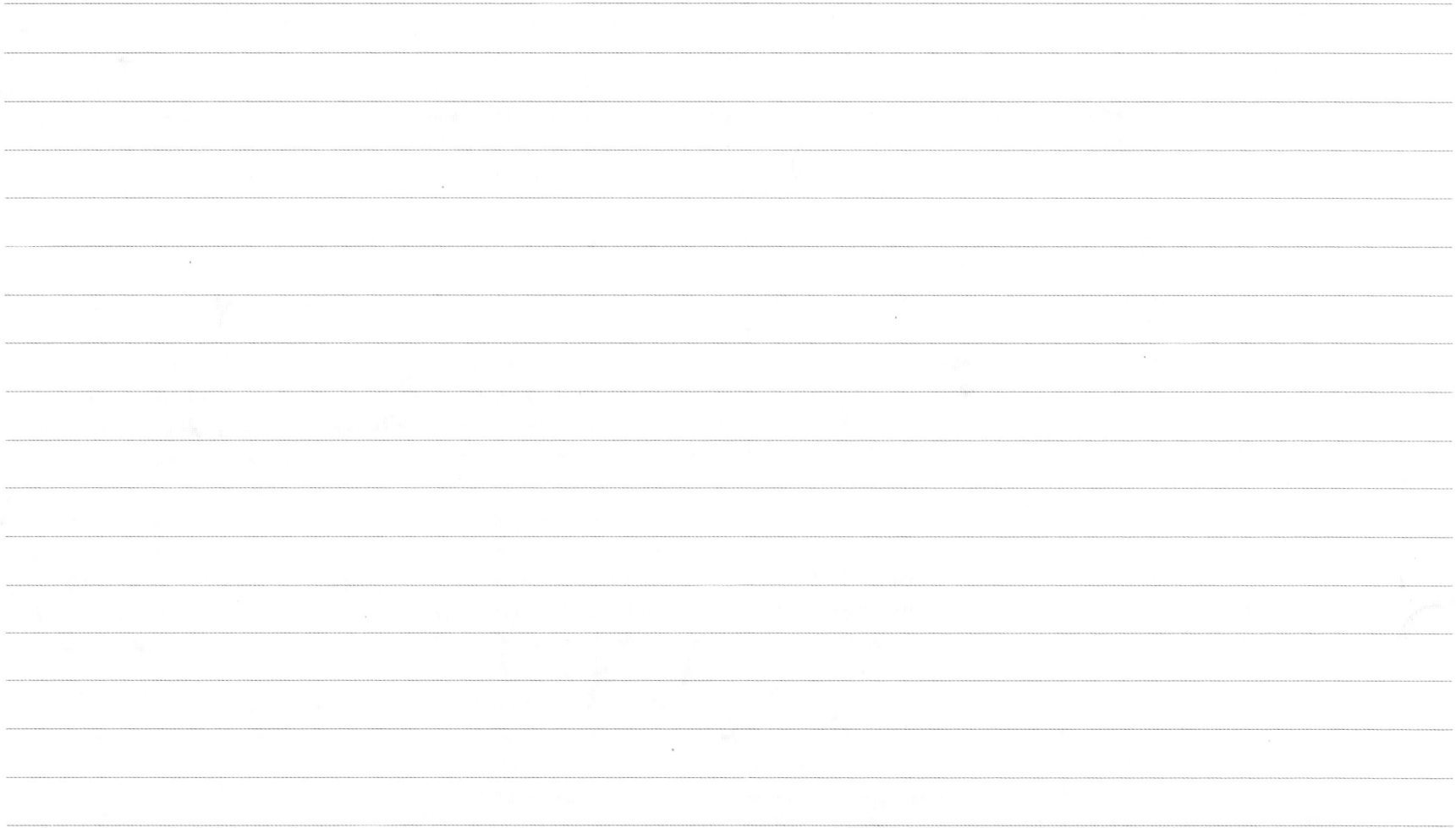

They lived quite a bit on fish. They dried whatever they got.

In those days people that were fishing would put them

on drying racks. I used to help my grandmother. They just

sliced 'em in two and hung 'em on the rack and smoked them.

They saved that for winter.

— Eneas Vanderburg, 2006

Aay
(large bull trout)

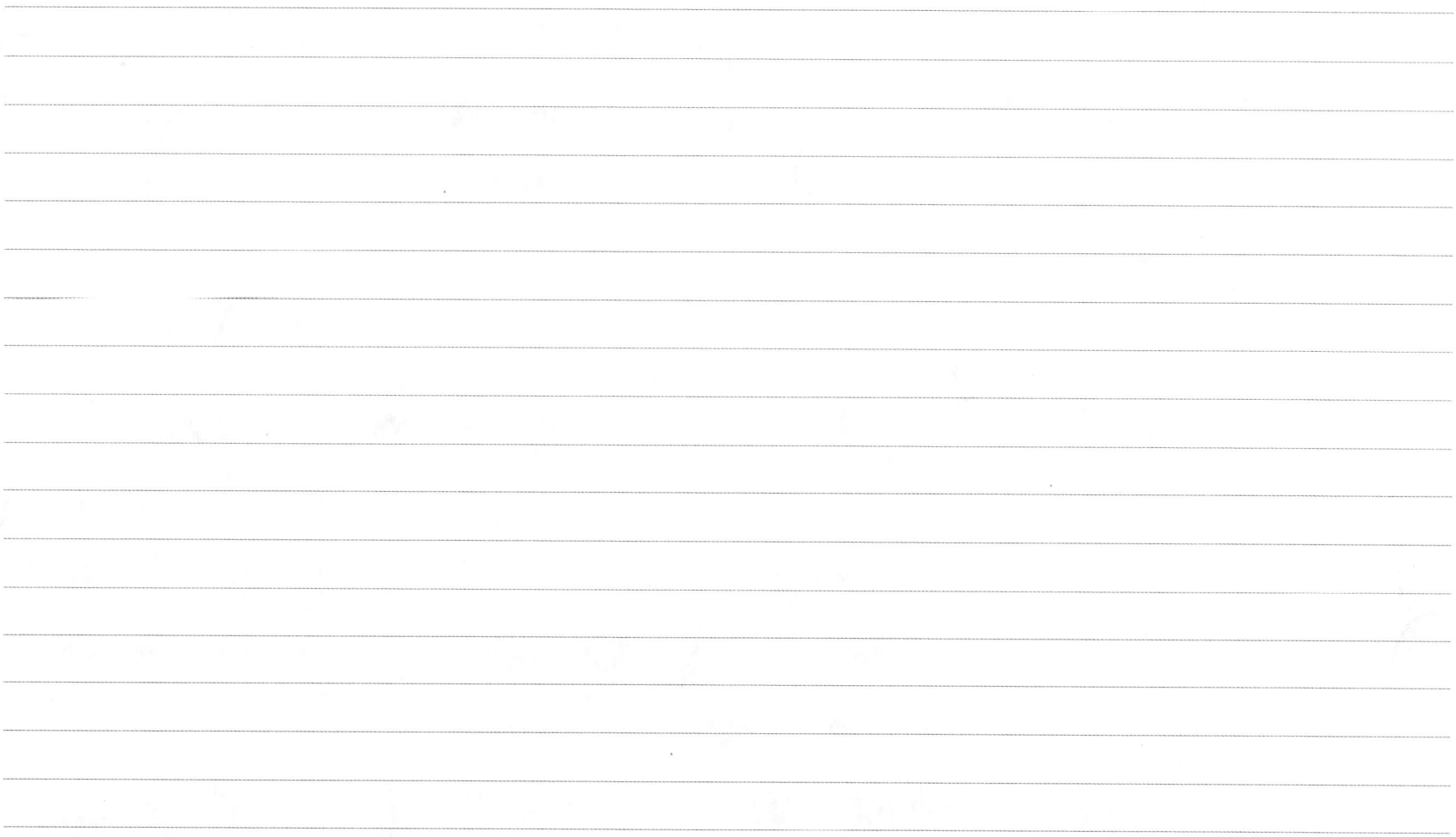

Our medicines must have water. It is from the winter [snow] that
the water flows from there to the lower parts of the land to the
medicinal plants gathered by the Indians.
The medicines, the food, have to have water.

— Mary "Dolly" Linsebigler, 2006

Čťú

(fishing line)

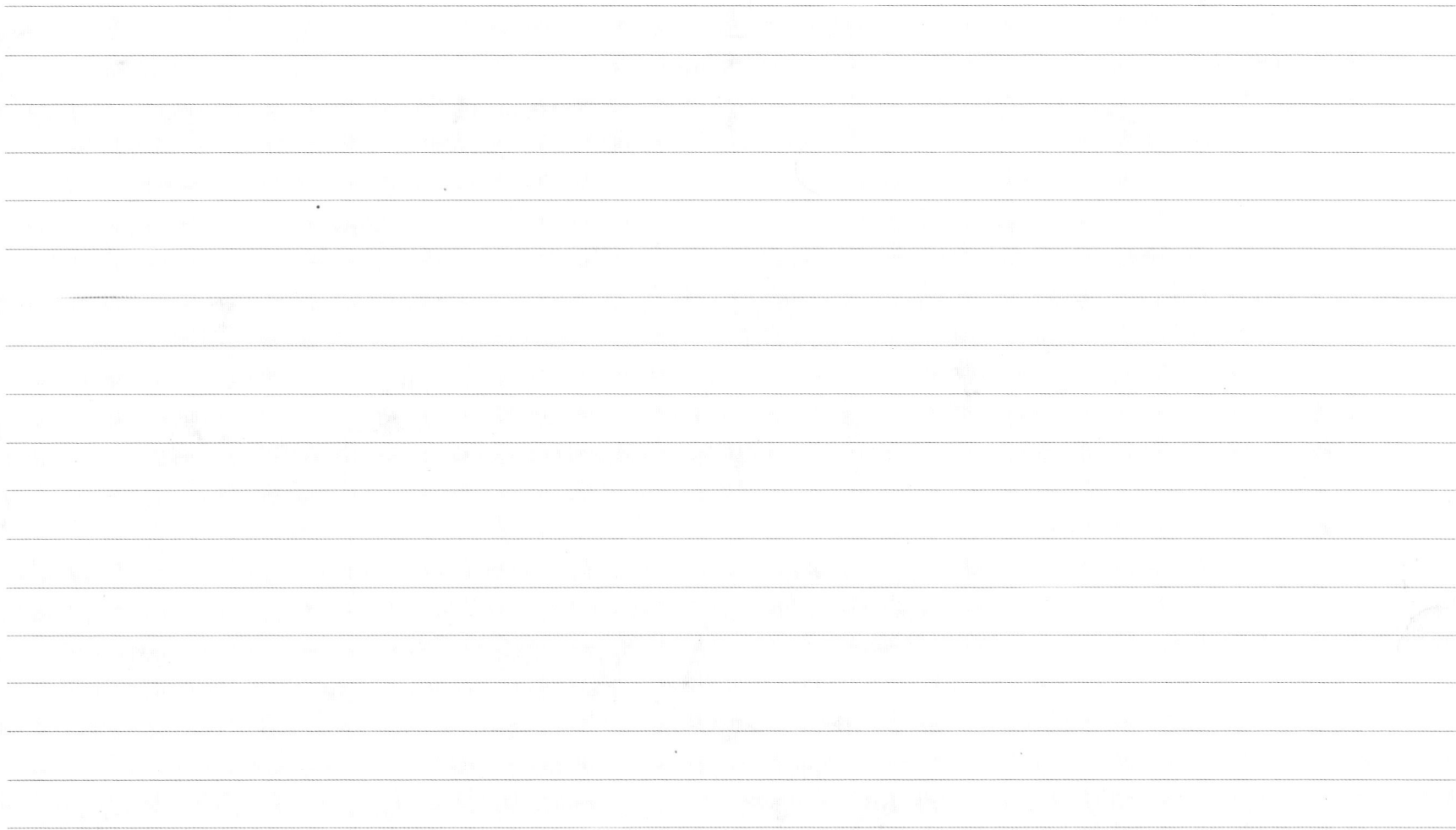

That's how Missoula got its name, Nɫʔay.

There used to be a lot of bull trout there.

— Pat Pierre, 2006

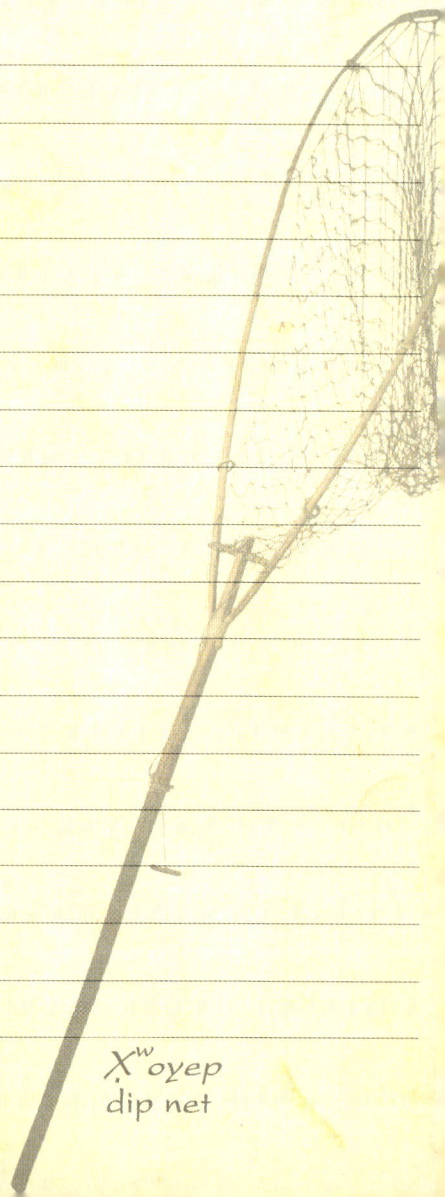

X̣ʷoɣep
dip net

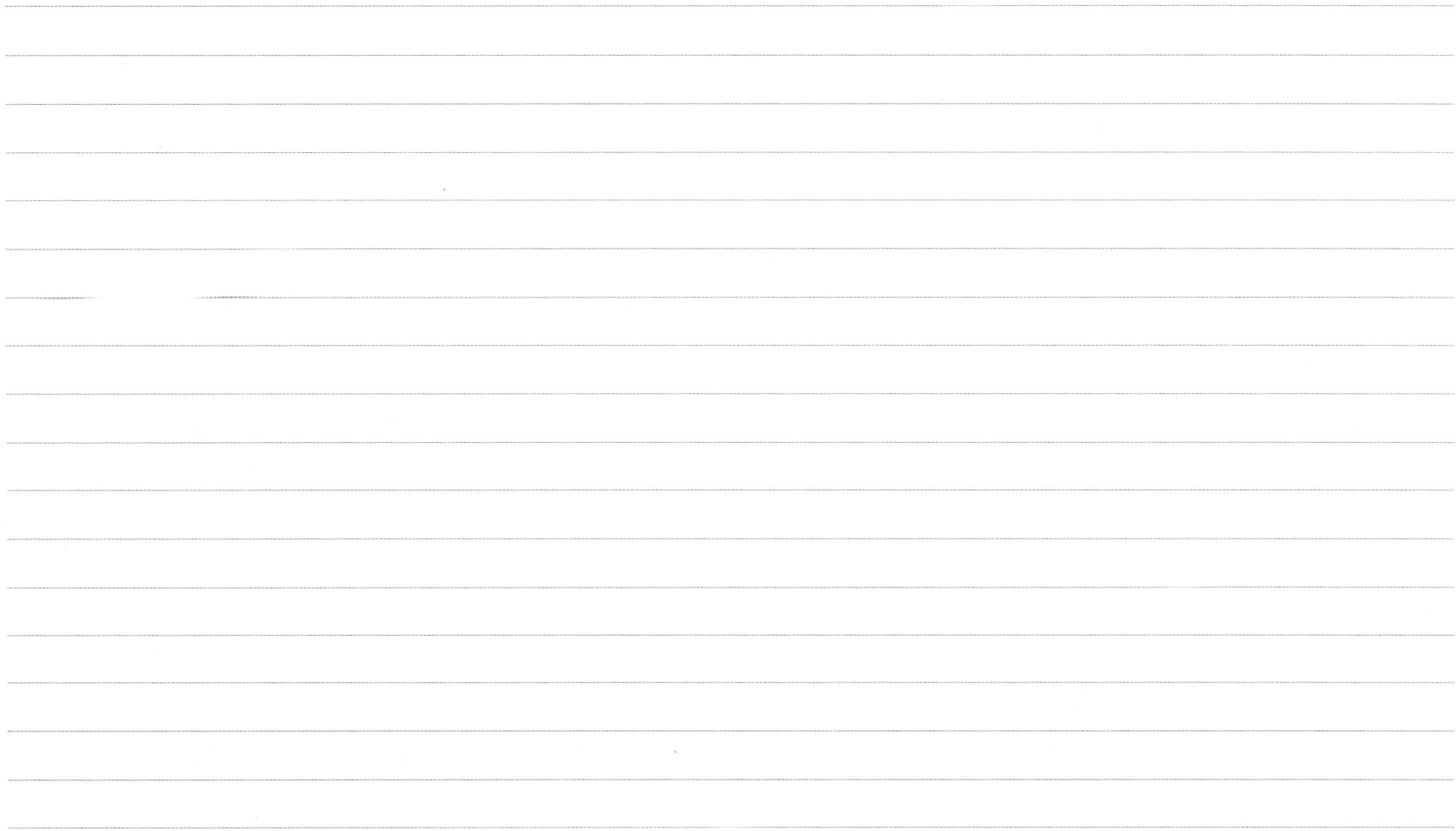

Whenever we wish, then we gather the fish. We find joy in that.

We are glad that we eat our animals, the fish and whatever

animals that live in the water. See, how good that is...

The Indians found joy in the water a long time ago.

This water is a place of play for the Indians. They...swam, bathed,

and did other things. The water is important to us.

— Mitch Smallsalmon, 1978

(Salish-Pend d'Oreille Culture Committee)

Pronunciation Guide for the Salish and Pend d'Oreille Dialects
as Written in the International Phonetic Alphabet
January 2010

Salish-Pend d'Oreille Alphabet

Aa Áá Cc Ċċ Čč Č̓č̓ Ee Éé Hh Ii Íí Kk K̓k̓ K̓ʷk̓ʷ K̓ʷk̓ʷ Ll Łł L̓l̓ Ļļ X̌ƛ̓
Mm M̓m̓ Ṃṃ Nn N̓n̓ Ṇṇ Oo Óó Pp P̓p̓ Qq Q̓q̓ Qʷqʷ Q̓ʷq̓ʷ Ss Šš Tt T̓t̓ Uu Úú
Ww W̓w̓ X̣x̣ Xx X̣x̣ X̌ʷx̌ʷ X̌ʷx̌ʷ Yy   Y̓ẏ ?

The Vowels

a   the vowel sound in the English words far, car, and are.

e   the vowel sound in the English words end, yes, and wed. If there is an e at the end of a word, it must be
        pronounced. In Salish, every letter is always pronounced; there are no silent e's in any words.

i   the vowel sound in the English words see and week.

o   a sound in between the vowel sounds in the English words road and bought.

u   the vowel sound in the English words cool, moo, and boo.

The Stops

c   a sound similar to the English ts sound at the end of the words cats and rats.

č   the soft ch sound in the English word church.

k   the k sound in the English word key.

k^w the k sound pronounced with the mouth rounded. It is similar to the start of the English word quick, but is made slightly further forward in the mouth.

p   a sound like the English p in the words paper and people.

q   a sound similar to the k sound, but pronounced farther back in the mouth or throat.

q^w the q sound pronounced with the mouth rounded. It is similar to the start of the English word queen, but is made slightly farther back in the mouth or throat.

t   the t sound in the English words to, hot, and at.

The Glottalized Stops

ċ   the c (ts) sound pronounced with glottalization (harder).

č̓   the č (ch) sound pronounced with glottalization.

k̓ʷ   the kʷ sound pronounced with glottalization.

λ̓   a clicking type of sound that combines the t̓ and I sounds. This is called a lambda.

p̓   the p sound pronounced with glottalization, producing a slight pop.

q̓   the q sound pronounced with glottalization.

q̓ʷ   the q̓ sound pronounced with the mouth rounded.

t̓   the t sound pronounced with glottalization, producing a slight pop.

The Fricatives

s   the s sound in the English words say and yes.

š   the sh sound in the English words shut, push, and wish.

h   the h sound in the English word hot.

ł   a sound made by pushing air along the sides of the mouth with the tongue behind the teeth. It is called a barred L or an unvoiced L.

x̣   a friction-like sound produced in the same area of the mouth as the q. (To learn this sound, begin by producing a sound much like softly clearing the throat.)

x̣ʷ   the x̣ sound made with the mouth rounded.

xʷ   the wh sound in the English word whoosh made with the mouth rounded.

The Resonants

l   a sound similar to the English l.

m   a sound like the English m.

n   a sound like the English n.

w   a sound like the English w.

y   a sound like the English y in the words yes, pay, and yarn.

The Glottalized Resonants

ỉ   the l sound pronounced with glottalization.

ṁ   the m sound pronounced with glottalization.

ṅ   the n sound pronounced with glottalization.

ẇ   the w sound pronounced with glottalization.

ẏ   the y sound pronounced with glottalization.

The Glottal Stop

?   a sound made by simply closing and opening the vocal chords. It abruptly cuts off or starts a sound, and is used before or after a vowel in some words. It is similar to the break in the middle of the English expression uh-huh, indicating no.

Long Vowels and Long Consonants

In words with double consonants, each consonant is pronounced separately.

In words with double vowels, each vowel is pronounced separately. This pronunciation makes the vowel sound longer.

Notes